CW00509590

Module B1 — Understanding Ourselves

Pages 1-2 — Fitness and Blood Pressure

Q1 systolic, higher, diastolic, lower, mmHg
Q2 E.g. poor circulation / dizziness / fainting
Q3 a) 24
   b) Dave is more likely to have high blood pressure because he has a stressful job and Tricia is retired / he smokes and Tricia doesn't / he consumes a lot more alcohol than Tricia every week.
   c) E.g. burst blood vessels / strokes / brain damage / kidney damage.
Q4 Petunia is wrong. Being healthy means being free from disease. But being fit is a measure of how well you can perform physical tasks.
Q5 a) A — Measuring oxygen uptake during exercise
   b) The ability of the heart to supply the muscles with oxygen.
   c) E.g. any three from: strength, speed, flexibility, agility.
Q6 E.g. any two from: He could reduce his weight. / He could eat a balanced diet. / He could do regular exercise.

Page 3 — High Blood Pressure and Heart Disease

Q1 plaques, restricting, thrombosis, oxygen, heart attack
Q2 a) saturated fat
   b) The cholesterol can form plaques, which restrict the flow of blood through arteries. This can lead to a heart attack.
Q3 A diet high in salt can cause high blood pressure, which damages the walls of arteries. This can lead to the formation of plaques, which can restrict blood flow and eventually cause a heart attack.
Q4 Nicotine — this chemical increases heart rate. The heart contracts more often and blood pressure is increased. Carbon monoxide — this chemical combines with haemoglobin in the red blood cells. This reduces the amount of oxygen the red blood cells can carry to the tissues. To make up for this, the heart has to contract more often, increasing blood pressure.

Page 4 — Eating Healthily

Q1 Carbohydrate — Simple sugars
Protein — Amino acids
Fat — Glycerol, Fatty acids
Q2

Nutrient	Storage in the body
Carbohydrate	Stored in the liver as glycogen or converted to fats
Protein	Not stored in the body
Fat	Stored under the skin and around organs as adipose tissue

Q3 a) Amino acids which can't be made by the body.
   b) Proteins which come from animals.
Q4 Wendy needs more carbohydrate and protein in her diet because she is more physically active. She needs more protein for muscle development and more carbohydrate for energy.
Q5 a) E.g. they might be intolerant to a food / they might be allergic to a food.
   b) E.g. they might think it's cruel to eat animals / they might think it's healthier not to eat meat / they might not like the taste of meat / they might think it's trendy not to eat meat.

Page 5 — Diet I

Q1 a) Developing countries are often overpopulated. little protein-rich food to go around.
There's not a lot of money to invest in agriculture in developing countries.
   b) $0.6 \times 75 = $ **45 g**
   c) i) E.g. teenagers need more protein than adults because they're still growing.
     ii) Women need extra protein during pregnancy to help their babies grow.
Q2 a) E.g. any two from: low self esteem / a poor self-image / a desire for perfection.
   b) E.g. any three from: liver failure / kidney failure / heart attacks / muscle wastage / low blood pressure / mineral deficiencies / tooth decay.
Q3 a) BMI = $76 \div (1.7)^2 = 76 \div 2.89 = $ **26.3**
   b) overweight

Page 6 — Infectious Disease

Q1 a) protozoan, parasite, host, vector, blood, infected
   b) i) E.g. people can be protected from mosquitoes using insecticides / mosquito nets.
     ii) E.g. fish can be introduced into the water to eat mosquito larvae / water where mosquitoes breed can be drained / sprayed with insecticide.
Q2 a) By damaging cells or producing toxins.
   b) They recognise the antigens on the surface of the pathogen.
   c) Yes, because antibodies are always specific so they won't be effective against the new cold pathogen.

Pages 7-8 — Preventing and Treating Infectious Disease

Q1 a) i) True
     ii) True
     iii) False
     iv) False
   b) antibodies, another organism, permanent, temporary
Q2 a) E.g. it protects you from disease. / If most people in a community are immunised it stops the disease spreading.
   b) E.g. there may be some short-term side effects such as redness, swelling or mild illness.
Q3 When John was immunised, he was given some dead/ inactive rubella pathogens that had antigens on their surfaces. John's white blood cells learnt to make antibodies specific to these antigens and some then remained in the blood as memory cells. When John was exposed to the rubella virus, the memory cells produce antibodies to destroy the virus before it infected him. James doesn't have these memory cells so the rubella virus can infect him and make him ill.
Q4 a) False
   b) True
   c) True
Q5 a) Antibiotics are only effective against bacterial infections.
   b) antivirals
They won't have any effect on Rachel's illness.
Q6 a) 9 days
   b) To prevent the emergence of antibiotic-resistant bacteria.

Page 9 — Cancer and Drug Development

Q1 a) In a benign tumour the cancerous cells do not spread to other sites in the body, but in malignant tumours they can do.
   b) E.g. any two from: giving up smoking / eating less processed meat / eating more fibre

Module B1 — Understanding Ourselves

Q2 1 — Computer models simulate a response to the drug
2 — Drug is tested on human tissue
3 — Drug is tested on live animals
4 — Human volunteers are used to test the drug

Q3 a) A placebo is a pill that looks like a drug being tested but doesn't do anything.

b) They use a placebo to make sure it is the actual drug which is causing any effects. Some patients will have beneficial effects just because they think they are receiving medicine.

c) A double blind trial is one where neither the scientist doing the test nor the patient knows whether they are getting a drug or a placebo.

Page 10 — Drugs: Use and Harm

Q1 a) A substance which alters the way the body works.

b) It means that the body has a physical need for the drug and the person will suffer withdrawal symptoms if no drug is given.

c) The body gets used to the drug and higher doses are needed to produce any / the same effect.

Q2

Type of drug	Example	Effects
Depressants	Alcohol / Temazepan / Solvents	Decrease the activity of the brain
Painkillers	Paracetamol	Reduce the number of 'painful' stimuli at the nerve endings near an injury
Stimulants	Nicotine / Ecstasy / Caffeine	Increase the activity of the brain
Performance enhancers	Anabolic steroids	Help athletes build muscles and train harder
Hallucinogens	LSD	Distort what is seen and heard by altering the pathways that the brain sends messages along

Q3 a) Paul, because he supplied the drugs and this is usually given greater punishment than using drugs.

b) Janice, because the drug she used (ketamine) is a class C drug, which is less dangerous and has lighter penalties than the class B drugs that Paul and Duncan took.

Pages 11-12 — Smoking and Alcohol

Q1 a) E.g. cancer / emphysema / heart disease / smoker's cough

b) Women who smoke often give birth to underweight babies.

Q2 Alcohol is broken down by enzymes in the liver and some of the products are toxic. If you drink too much alcohol over a long period of time these toxic products can cause the death of liver cells, forming scar tissue that stops blood reaching the liver — this is called cirrhosis.

Q3 a) 3 + 3 = **6 units**.

b) Yes. 1 unit = at least 20 mg per 100 cm³.
20 × 6 = 120 mg per 100 cm³. This is more than the legal limit of 80 mg per 100 cm³.

c) E.g. because your reactions are slower / your coordination is poor / your judgement is impaired.

Q4 a) False
b) False
c) True

Q5 a) 70%

b) The number of male smokers aged 35-54 has been decreasing since 1950. The number of female smokers aged 35-54 rose between 1950 and 1970, but then it began to decrease. The number of male smokers aged 35-54 has been consistently greater than the number of female smokers aged 35-54.

c) Smoking damages the cilia of the epithelial tissue lining the trachea, bronchi and bronchioles. This encourages mucus to be produced, but because the cilia are damaged this mucus can't be cleared. As a result, it sticks to air passages and causes smoker's cough.

Pages 13-14 — Receptors — The Eye

Q1

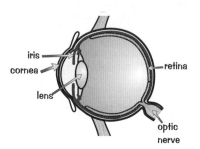

Q2

Part of the eye	Function
Lens	Focuses light on the retina
Optic nerve	Carries impulses from the eye to the brain
Retina	Contains light receptors
Ciliary muscles	Causes the lens to change shape
Iris	Controls how much light enters the pupil

Q3 elastic, accommodation, relaxes, tighten, less rounded, less

Q4 near, short, convex, distant, long, concave, corneal laser surgery

Q5 a) The brain compares the images of an object seen by each eye. The more similarities there are between the images, the further away the object is.

b) It gives a narrow field of vision.

Q6 a) retina

b) It's caused by a lack of certain specialised (cone) cells in the retina.

Page 15 — Neurones and Reflexes

Q1 a) quickly
b) protect
c) without
d) reflex arc

Q2 1 - stimulus, 2 - receptor, 3 - sensory neurone, 4 - relay neurone, 5 - motor neurone, 6 - effector, 7 - response.

Q3 a) It travels as an electrical impulse along the axon.

b) This allows the neurone to connect up with many others.

c) It insulates the axon. This speeds up the impulse.

Q4 a) It is carried across by a chemical transmitter.

b) Stimulant drugs increase the amount of transmitter chemical at some synapses, which increases the frequency of impulses along the second neurone.

GCSE

Biology

Exam Board: OCR Gateway

For the **New 2011** **GCSE Science** courses

Answer Book

Higher Level

Contents

Module B1 — Understanding Ourselves.............................. 3

Module B2 — Understanding Our Environment 7

Module B3 — Living and Growing......................... 10

Module B4 — It's a Green World........................ 13

Module B5 — The Living Body........................... 17

Module B6 — Beyond the Microscope................................ 21

Published by CGP

ISBN: 978 1 84762 611 0

Groovy website: www.cgpbooks.co.uk

Printed by Elanders Ltd, Newcastle upon Tyne.
Jolly bits of clipart from CorelDRAW®

Based on the classic CGP style created by Richard Parsons.

Module B1 — Understanding Ourselves

Page 16 — Homeostasis

Q1 Homeostasis is the maintenance of a constant internal environment in the body.

Q2 counteracts, lowers, optimum

Q3 a) the brain / the thermoregulatory centre

b) 37 °C is the optimum temperature for enzymes controlling reactions in the human body. The enzymes don't work as well if the temperature varies too much from the optimum.

c) i) E.g. heat stroke / dehydration

ii) E.g. hypothermia

Q4 a) When sweat evaporates it uses heat from your skin. This transfers heat from your skin to the environment, cooling you down.

b) i) Vasodilation is the widening of blood vessels. Vasoconstriction is the constriction of the blood vessels.

ii) Vasodilation and vasoconstriction allow the body to control the blood flow near the surface of the skin. This allows the body to lose or retain heat in response to the environmental temperature.

Pages 17-18 — Controlling Blood Sugar Level

Q1 a) from food containing carbohydrate

b) i) insulin

ii) liver

Q2 insulin, pancreas, insulin, liver, glucose, blood, reduced / lower.

Q3 Nervous messages are transmitted as electrical impulses and travel directly to effectors. Hormones travel in the blood, so can take longer to reach their target organ.

Q4 a) It's a condition where the pancreas produces little or no insulin.

b) By injecting insulin at mealtimes / avoiding foods rich in simple carbohydrates/sugars

c) The insulin causes the glucose in Ruby's blood to be removed by the liver so the blood glucose level falls.

d) Yes — vigorous exercise removes a lot of glucose from the blood, so she will have to use less insulin.

Q5 a) It's a condition where a person's body cells become resistant to insulin and don't respond properly to it.

b) By avoiding foods that are rich in simple carbohydrates/ sugars.

Pages 19-20 — Plant Hormones and Growth

Q1 a) False

b) False

c) True

d) True

Q2 shade, faster, towards, positively, shade, slower, away from, negatively

Q3 a) Auxin moves through the plant in solution.

b) i) shoot will bend towards the right

ii) shoot will grow straight up

c) i) The auxin diffuses into the cells on the left hand side of the shoot, making only these cells elongate and causing the shoot to grow towards the right.

ii) The auxin diffuses into all the cells at the top of the cut shoot, making all the cells elongate. The shoot would grow straight upwards.

Q4 a) auxins

b) At the tips of the shoots and roots.

c) i) In the shoot, auxin moves towards the lower side of the shoot where it stimulates growth — so the shoot bends upwards, against gravity. The shoot is negatively geotropic.

ii) In the root, auxin moves to the lower side of the root, where it inhibits growth, making the root grow downwards, in the same direction as gravity. The root is positively geotropic.

Q5 Seedling A: the foil prevents any light reaching the tip, so the auxin is evenly distributed in the tip and no bending occurs.
Seedling C: the mica strip prevents the auxin from moving to the side that's in the shade, so there is even distribution of auxin and no bending occurs.

Page 21 — Commercial Use of Plant Hormones

Q1 E.g. as selective weedkillers / growing cuttings with rooting powder / controlling the ripening of fruit / controlling dormancy.

Q2 a) E.g. unripe fruit is firmer, so it's less easily damaged during picking and transport.

b) i) E.g. they can be sprayed with a ripening hormone.

ii) During transport to the market.

Q3 a) A period during which seeds will not germinate until they've been through certain conditions.

b) E.g. it would ensure that all the seeds would germinate at the same time. It means that seeds can be made to germinate at times of the year when they wouldn't normally.

Page 22 — Genes and Chromosomes

Q1 nucleus, chromosomes, DNA, gene

Q2 gene, chromosome, nucleus, cell

Q3 a) False

b) True

c) True

d) False

Q4 'Alleles' are different forms of the same gene.

Page 23 — Genetic Variation

Q1

	Can cause variation	Does not cause variation
Formation of gametes from reproductive cells	✓	
Mutation of a reproductive cell	✓	
Random fertilisation	✓	
Conditions in the womb when the baby is developing	✓	
Environmental effects after birth	✓	

Q2 4 — It's hard to say if your genes or your environment are more important for characteristics like intelligence.

Q3 a) i) Gametes are sex cells, e.g. sperm and eggs.

ii) When cells in an individual's testes/ovaries split to form gametes, some of its father's chromosomes are grouped with some from its mother. This shuffling of chromosomes in the gametes leads to variation in the new generation.

b) Fertilisation is random — you don't know which two gametes are going to join together.

c) The gametes have 23 chromosomes so that when two gametes join together during fertilisation the resulting fertilised cell will have the full number of chromosomes.

Module B1 — Understanding Ourselves

Pages 24-25 — Genetic Diagrams

Q1 a) no
b) In a genetic diagram, the allele for a dominant characteristic is a capital letter (e.g. R) and the allele for a recessive characteristic is a lower case letter (e.g. r).
c) homozygous
Q2 a) i) red eyes
ii) white eyes
iii) red eyes
iv) white eyes
b) i)

	parent's alleles	
	R	**r**
R	RR	**Rr**
r	**Rr**	**rr**

(left axis label: parent's alleles)

ii) 25% (0.25, 1 in 4, ¼)
iii) There are most likely to be 72 with red eyes (three quarters).
Q3 Genotype — The genetic makeup of an organism.
Phenotype — The characteristics expressed by an organism.
Q4 a)

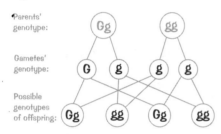

b) 1 : 1 (half grey, half white)
c) 6 grey mice, 6 white mice.
Q5 Sally can cross the plants. If the red-flowered plant is RR then all their offspring will be red. If the red-flowered plant is Rr then there will be an approximate 3 : 1 ratio of red to white offspring.

Pages 26-27 — Sex Inheritance and Genetic Disorders

Q1 a) True
b) False
c) True
d) False
Q2 a)

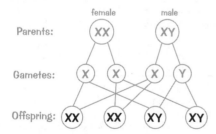

b) 50% (1 in 2, 0.5, ½)
c) Sarah's wrong. It is most likely that half (four) of the children will be boys, but this is only a probability — in reality it might be more or less because there is a 50% chance of having a boy with each pregnancy.
Q3 a) i) 1
ii) 2

b)

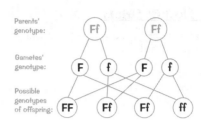

c) i) 25% (1 in 4, 0.25, ¼)
ii) 50% (1 in 2, 0.5, ½)
Q4 a) E.g. The parents might not be able to cope with a sick or disabled child.
b) E.g. A baby with a genetic disorder has just as much right to life as a healthy baby.

Pages 28-30 — Mixed Questions — Module B1

Q1 a) amino acids
b) Proteins are not stored in the body.
c) kwashiorkor
d) The woman who is breast feeding will have a higher EAR of protein than a woman who isn't breast feeding. This is because she will need to extra protein to produce milk.
Q2 a) No, because antibiotics only kill bacteria and fungi.
b) i) Using a computer model / human tissue
ii) E.g. because it's cruel to test drugs on animals.
iii) A blind trial is where the patient in the study doesn't know whether they're getting the drug being tested or a placebo (a pill that doesn't do anything).
Q3 a) pancreas
b) glycogen
c) The diagram shows how a rise or fall in blood glucose will trigger a response that counteracts the change.
Q4 a) 2 — Red-green colour blindness results from a lack of specialised cone cells in the retina.
b) i) Alleles are different versions of the same gene.
ii) When there's no dominant allele of the gene present.
Q5 a) Cigarette smoke contains carcinogens (chemicals which cause cancer).
b) i) A tumour that grows and can spread to other sites in the body.
ii) E.g. by not smoking
Q6 Recessive, because the parents carry the allele, but do not show albinism themselves.
Q7 a) In humans, the males have two different sex chromosomes but in chickens they have two copies of the same sex chromosome.
b)

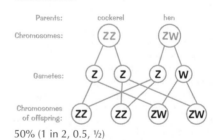

c) 50% (1 in 2, 0.5, ½)

Module B2 — Understanding Our Environment

Module B2 — Understanding Our Environment

Page 31 — Classification

Q1 a) i) phylum
ii) order
iii) genus
b) Natural classification systems are based on the evolutionary relationships and genetic similarities between organisms. Artificial ones are based on appearance rather than genes and are used to identify organisms.
c) Because many organisms share characteristics of multiple groups.
Q2 species, classification, adapted, sequencing, genetic, related
Q3

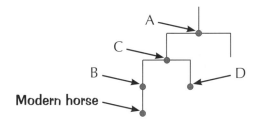

Page 32 — Species

Q1 a) A species is a group of organisms which can interbreed to produce fertile offspring.
b) Binomial means a two-part name (one name for the genus and one for the species).
c) *sapiens*
Q2 Hybrids are usually infertile. This means they can't interbreed, so they don't fit the definition of a species.
Q3 Organisms that reproduce asexually don't interbreed. This means they don't fit the definition of a species.
Q4 a) The more recent the common ancestor of two species, the more closely related they are.
b) Llamas and camels look very different as they've developed features that make them well adapted to survive in very different environments.

Page 33 — Pyramids of Biomass and Numbers

Q1 a)

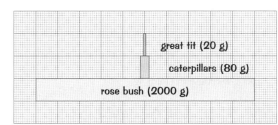

b) One rose bush would feed a large number of caterpillars, so in a pyramid of numbers for this food chain the caterpillars bar would be longer than the rose bush bar.
Q2 a) i) Dry biomass is the mass of the organisms after all the water has been dried out of them.
ii) It's difficult because you have to kill the organisms to work it out.
b) E.g. some organisms can feed at more than one trophic level.

Pages 34-35 — Energy Transfer and Energy Flow

Q1 a) energy
b) Plants, photosynthesis
c) eat
d) respiration
e) lost, heat
Q2 a) Grain = 50 000 kJ
Mouse = 8000 kJ
Owl = 500 kJ
b) i) 50 000 − 8000 = **42 000 kJ**
ii) 8000 − 500 = **7500 kJ**
c) i) (8000 ÷ 50 000) × 100 = **16%**
ii) (500 ÷ 8000) × 100 = **6.25%**
Q3 a) (2070 ÷ 103 500) × 100 = **2%**
b) 2070 ÷ 10 = **207**
207 − (90 + 100) = **17 kJ**
c) E.g. any two from: heat loss / egestion / excretion
d) So much energy is lost at each stage of a food chain that there's not enough left to support more organisms after about five stages.
Q4 a) 3
b) 30 000 kJ
c) 5000 − 100 = **4900 kJ**
Q5 a) i) 100 000 − 90 000 = **10 000 kJ**
ii) (10 000 ÷ 100 000) × 100 = **10%**
b) i) 5 ÷ 100 × 1000 = **50 kJ**
ii) 1000 − 50 = **950 kJ**
c) Energy is stored in the food chain as biomass. Energy transfer between trophic levels isn't very efficient, so some is lost at each stage. This means biomass is smaller at each trophic level.

Pages 36-37 — Interactions Between Organisms

Q1 a) Because they're competing for similar ecological niches.
b) i) Interspecific
ii) Intraspecific
iii) bigger
Q2 An ecological niche is how a species fits in to its ecosystem. It depends on things like where the individuals live and what they feed on.
Q3 a) Predator: heron
Prey: frog
b) The number of frogs will decrease.
c) E.g. increase in number of herons / lack of food
d) If the number of frogs decreases then the number of herons will fall because there is less food (frogs) for them.
e) It takes a while for one population to respond to changes in the other population.
Q4 a) flea and tapeworm
b) In a parasitic relationship, parasites live off a host but give nothing back. In mutualism, both organisms benefit.
c) i) E.g. the 'cleaner' animals, like the oxpecker birds found on the backs of buffalo.
ii) E.g. both organisms benefit — the oxpeckers get food and the buffalo get pests removed from their skin and coat.
iii) E.g. The number of oxpeckers is likely to fall if the number of buffalos falls because the oxpeckers rely on the buffalo for food.
Q5 a) interspecific
b) intraspecific
c) Two barn owls will have exactly the same needs, so will compete for more resources than a barn owl and a fox, who will only compete for food.

Module B2 — Understanding Our Environment

Page 38 — Adaptations

Q1 a) Adaptations are features of an organism that make it better suited to its environment.

b) They need to adapt so they are better able to compete for limited resources — making them more likely to survive and reproduce.

Q2 a) specialists
b) generalists
c) specialists, generalists
d) generalists, specialists

Q3 a) extremophiles, enzymes, optimum, denature
b) Proteins that interfere with the formation and growth of ice crystals in an organism's cells.

Page 39 — Adaptations to Cold Environments

Q1 a) E.g. a layer of blubber
b) small surface area to volume ratio
c) Their small surface area to volume ratio means that less heat is lost through the surface of the skin, reducing heat loss to the environment.

Q2 a) The arteries and veins flowing to and from the feet are close to each other, allowing heat to transfer between them. Warm blood in the arteries heats cold blood returning from the feet. This stops the cold blood from cooling down the rest of the body.
b) E.g. penguins

Q3 Hibernation saves energy as the animals don't have to find food or keep themselves as warm as if they were active.

Page 40 — Adaptations to Hot and Dry Environments

Q1 a) reduce, increase
b) a behavioural
c) gain from
d) large

Q2 E.g. Having large ears increases the elephants' surface area to volume ratio, helping them to lose heat.

Q3 a) E.g. specialised kidneys / no sweat glands / spend lots of time in moist underground burrows
b) i) E.g. rounded shape / thick waxy cuticle / spines instead of leaves / store water in their leaves / extensive roots
ii) E.g. rounded shape reduces surface area to volume ratio to minimise water loss / waxy cuticle reduces water loss / spines reduce water loss / storing water allows them to survive when water is unavailable / extensive roots mean water is absorbed over a large area

Page 41 — Evolution and Speciation

Q1
1. All giraffes had short necks.
2. The giraffes competed for food from low branches. This food started to become scarce. Many giraffes died before they could breed.
3. A giraffe was born with a longer neck than normal. The long-necked giraffe was able to eat more food.
4. The long-necked giraffe survived to have lots of offspring that all had longer necks.
5. More long-necked giraffes survived to breed, so more giraffes were born with long necks.
6. All giraffes have long necks.

Q2 appeared, offspring, DNA, Successful, inherit

Q3 a) When populations can't interbreed to produce fertile offspring.

b) When populations are geographically isolated, they can't mix. Different mutations create different new features in the two populations. Natural selection works on the new features so that, if they are of benefit, they spread through each of the populations. Eventually, individuals from the two populations will become reproductively isolated.

Page 42 — Theories of Evolution

Q1 a) Lamarck said that if a characteristic is used a lot by an animal then it would become more developed. He said that acquired characteristics could be passed on to the offspring.
b) People realised that acquired characteristics don't have a genetic basis — so they can't be passed on to the next generation.

Q2 a) some religious people
b) Darwin's theory contradicted the views of people who believed that all species had been created as they are now, by God.

Q3 The theory's been debated and tested by lots of scientists, who couldn't prove it to be wrong. / It offers a plausible explanation for many observations of plants and animals.

Pages 43-44 — The Carbon Cycle and Decomposition

Q1 a) b) c)

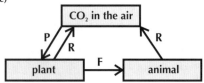

Q2 a) photosynthesis
b) carbon dioxide
c) glucose (then carbohydrates, proteins and fats)
d) by animals feeding on other organisms
e) respiration

Q3 a) i) It would be slower in a waterlogged soil.
ii) Waterlogged soils contain less oxygen. Decomposers need oxygen to respire and release energy. As there's less oxygen, they have less energy and work more slowly. This means carbon is recycled more slowly.
b) Extremely acidic conditions will slow down the reproduction of decomposers or even kill them, slowing the rate of carbon recycling.

Q4 carbon dioxide, carbon sinks, carbonates, limestone, volcanic eruptions, atmosphere

Q5 a) fossil fuel (accept coal or oil)
b) Fossil fuels are formed from dead animals and plants which contain carbon.
c) combustion / burning

Page 45 — The Nitrogen Cycle

Q1 Plants — By absorbing nitrates from the soil
Animals — By eating other organisms
Decomposers — By breaking down dead organisms and animal waste

Q2 a) Decomposers — Decompose proteins and urea into ammonia.
b) Nitrifying bacteria — Turn ammonia into nitrates which plants can use.
c) Denitrifying bacteria — Turn nitrates back into nitrogen gas.
d) Nitrogen-fixing bacteria — Turn nitrogen gas into nitrogen compounds that plants can use.

Module B2 — Understanding Our Environment

Q3 a) Lightning converting nitrogen from the air into nitrogen compounds in the soil.

b) Denitrifying bacteria converting nitrates in the soil into nitrogen gas.

Q4 a) Legume plants have root nodules that contain nitrogen-fixing bacteria. These bacteria convert nitrogen gas into nitrogen compounds, which plants can use.

b) Plants use the nitrogen compounds in the soil to make proteins for growth. More nitrogen compounds in the soil would mean increased plant growth.

Pages 46-47 — Human Impact on the Environment

Q1 a) Sulfur dioxide released when fossil fuels are burnt.

b) E.g. Sea level will rise. / Weather systems will become less predictable. / Agricultural output will fall.

c) A carbon footprint is the amount of greenhouse gases given off by a person, company or country in a certain period of time.

Q2 higher, exponentially, more, environment, resources, pollution, developed, higher, pollution, population

Q3 a) CFC gases (found in polystyrene, aerosols, air-conditioning units, fridges etc.)

b) UV rays that enter through the hole could be harmful to their skin / could increase their risk of skin cancer.

c) E.g. The UV rays could kill plankton in the ocean around Antarctica, causing fish levels to drop.

Q4 a) An indicator species.

b) Mayfly larvae prefer clean water and sludgeworms prefer water that contains sewage.

Q5 a) Site 1

b) Advantage: E.g. they allow reliable numerical data to be collected / exact pollutants to be identified.
Disadvantage: E.g. more expensive than living methods

c) i) Lichens

ii) E.g. They aren't always reliable methods for measuring pollution, as factors other than pollution can affect them.

Page 48 — Endangered Species

Q1 conservation, endangered, restrictions, ensuring, plants, extinct

Q2 a) When there are no more individuals of a species left.

b) It's hard for organisms to find resources like food and shelter if there aren't enough suitable habitats to support them.

Q3 a) It's important that species interact with each other as they would in their natural environment, e.g. predator species should be allowed to hunt prey.

b) Populations should be able to reproduce. They must contain both males and females of reproductive age, and should also be large enough to prevent inbreeding.

Page 49 — Sustainable Development

Q1 a) Sustainable development means providing for the needs of today's increasing population without harming the environment.

b) E.g. any two from: We need to produce more food — so we're using up more land for farming. / We're using more energy from sources like fossil fuels, which will eventually run out. / We're producing more waste, which is polluting the Earth and damaging the environment.

Q2 a) False
b) True
c) True
d) False
e) False
f) False

Q3 E.g. Fishing quotas have been introduced to prevent over-fishing.

Q4 Education makes people aware of the importance of sustainability and helps them to make sustainable choices, for example about the things they buy.

Pages 50-52 — Mixed Questions — Module B2

Q1 a) 1. A physical barrier divides a population of a species, e.g. a river changes its course.
2. Different mutations create different new features in the two groups of organisms.
3. Natural selection works on the features so that, if they are beneficial, they spread through each of the populations.
4. Eventually, the two populations will change so much that they become two separate, reproductively isolated species.

b) If genetic variation is low, then a species is less likely to be able to adapt to changes in the environment or survive the appearance of a new disease.

Q2 a) because they occupy the same ecological niche

b) Generalists are species that are adapted to survive in a range of habitats.

c) *Sciurus*

Q3 a) nitrogen-fixing bacteria

b) for growth and making proteins

c) Both organisms benefit from the relationship. The plant gets nitrogen compounds to make proteins and the bacteria get sugars from the plant.

Q4 a) i) 43 700 − 7500 = **36 200 kJ**
ii) 7500 ÷ 43 700 = **17%**

b) E.g. any two from: in heat from respiration / egestion / excretion.

c) E.g. Organisms such as decomposers feed on the waste products and start a new food chain.

d) A — respiration
B — feeding / ingestion / digestion
C — decomposition / decay
D — respiration by decomposers
E — photosynthesis
F — respiration

Q5 a) The second Latin name, which gives the species, is different for the two geese.

b) They belong to the same genus. / The first Latin name is the same.

c) i) the binomial system
ii) It means that scientists from different countries, or who speak different languages, can all refer to a particular species by the same name — avoiding confusion.

d) It helps us to understand how organisms are related (evolutionary relationships) and how they interact with each other (ecological relationships).

Q6 a) E.g. He could take direct measurements of pollution levels / he could look for indicator species in the water near to the factory. Water lice, rat-tailed maggots and sludgeworms are all indicators of polluted water.

b) i) E.g. plant trees to replace the ones they've felled to make the paper from.
ii) E.g. Sustainable development can help endangered species by considering the impacts on their habitats from activities such as logging.

Module B3 — Living and Growing

Module B3 — Living and Growing

Page 53 — Cells

Q1 a) i) Plant Cells, Animal Cells
ii) Bacterial Cells
iii) Plant Cells, Animal Cells
b) E.g. any two from: chloroplasts / nucleus / mitochondria
Q2 a) i) Mitochondria provide the cell with energy from respiration. The liver carries out energy-demanding metabolic reactions so it needs lots of mitochondria.
ii) E.g. muscle cells
b) i) Ribosomes are too small to be seen with a light microscope.
ii) the cytoplasm
iii) protein synthesis

Page 54 — DNA

Q1 chromosomes, genes, helix, bases, A/G, G/A, cross, complementary

Q2

A	C	T	G	C	A	A	T	G
T	G	A	C	G	T	T	A	C

Q3 1. The DNA double helix 'unzips' to form two single strands.
2. Bases on free-floating nucleotides pair up with complementary bases on the DNA.
3. Cross links form between the bases and the nucleotides are joined together.
4. Two double-stranded molecules of DNA are formed.

Q4 a) i) 2. X-ray data showing there were two chains of DNA wound in a helix.
ii) Data showing that the bases occurred in pairs.
b) E.g. other scientists need to repeat the work first to make sure the results are reliable.

Page 55 — Protein Synthesis

Q1 a) particular protein
b) a different
c) amino acids
d) three
Q2 functions, enzymes, full set, off, on
Q3 a) The number and order of amino acids gives a protein a particular shape and therefore a particular function.
b) by the sequence of bases in DNA
Q4 a) mRNA acts as a messenger between DNA and the ribosomes — it carries the code needed to make proteins between the two.
b) Proteins are made in the cell cytoplasm. DNA is in the cell nucleus and can't move out into the cytoplasm because it's too big, so a copy of the DNA is needed to make proteins (mRNA).

Page 56 — Functions of Proteins

Q1 insulin — hormone — regulates blood sugar level
haemoglobin — carrier molecule — transports oxygen around the body
collagen — structural protein — strengthens connective tissues
Q2 a) i) False
ii) True
iii) False
b) E.g. Enzymes speed up/catalyse chemical reactions in living cells.
Enzymes catalyse reactions involved with protein synthesis.

Q3 a) A substance that speeds up a reaction without being changed or used up in the reaction itself.
b) i) That enzymes usually only work with one substrate.
ii) For the enzyme to work the substrate has to fit into the active site. If the substrate doesn't match the active site's shape, then the reaction won't be catalysed.
c) E.g.

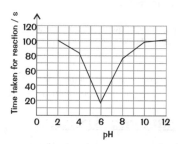

Pages 57-58 — More on Enzymes

Q1 a) 33 °C (allow 32 °C – 34 °C)
b) At low temperatures enzymes and substrate molecules have less energy. This means they move around less, so they're less likely to meet up and react (they have a lower collision rate).
c) Some of the bonds holding the enzyme together break, causing the enzyme to lose its shape. This means its active site won't fit the shape of the substrate anymore. The enzyme is denatured.
Q2 a) How much the rate of a reaction changes when the temperature is increased by 10 °C.
b) i) E.g. rate at 20 °C ÷ rate at 10 °C = 6 ÷ 2 = **3**
ii) The rate of reaction trebles when the temperature is increased by 10 °C.
Q3 a)

(graph: Time taken for reaction / s (y-axis, 0 to 120) against pH (x-axis, 0 to 12))

b) pH 6
c) At very high and very low pH levels the bonds in the enzymes are broken and the enzyme is denatured. The active site changes shape, meaning that it can't speed up the reaction.
d) No. This enzyme works very slowly at low pHs.
e) E.g. any two from: the temperature should be the same at each pH / the same volume of the reactant and enzyme should be used for each pH / the same method of determining when the reaction is complete should be used for each pH.

Page 59 — Mutations

Q1 a) i) False
ii) True
iii) True
iv) False
v) False
vi) True
b) E.g. Mutations are not always harmful.
Mutations can lead to the production of different proteins.
Mutations are changes to the DNA base sequence.
Q2 a) The explosion released radiation, which causes mutations that increase the chance of cancer.
b) Cigarette smoke contains chemicals that are known to cause mutations. These mutations increase the risk of developing cancer.

Module B3 — Living and Growing

Q3 A different protein could be produced after a mutation, which might be an improvement on the one it was supposed to be. This could give the organism a survival advantage.

Page 60 — Multiplying Cells

Q1 E.g. to produce cells for growth / repair

Q2 replicated, line up, centre, divide, opposite

Q3 a) E.g. Any two of: Multicellular organisms can be bigger which allows them to move further, get nutrients in different ways and fewer things can squash or eat them. / Being multicellular allows for cell differentiation. Instead of being just one cell that has to do everything, you can have different types of cells that are specialised to do different jobs. / Multicellular organisms can be more complex, so can be adapted to their particular environment.

b) i) a nervous system — to communicate between different cells.

ii) a respiratory system — to control the exchange of substances (gases) with the environment.

iii) a circulatory system — to supply cells with the nutrients they need.

Page 61 — Meiosis, Gametes and Fertilisation

Q1 egg/sperm, sperm/egg, meiosis, diploid, two copies, haploid, one copy

Q2 a) False

b) False

c) True

Q3 a) i) The pairs of chromosomes split up — the chromosomes in each pair are pulled to opposite poles of the cell.

ii) Each chromosome splits in half and one arm ends up in each new cell.

b) When the chromosomes are first pulled apart in meiosis, it creates a random mixture (assortment) of the father's and the mother's chromosomes, so each new cell is genetically different.

Q4 a) To provide energy needed to swim to an egg cell.

b) To release the enzymes they need to digest their way through the membrane of the egg cell.

Page 62 — Stem Cells, Differentiation and Growth

Q1 3. Undifferentiated cells that can develop into different types of cells, tissues and organs.

Q2 E.g. Any three from: Animals only tend to grow until they reach a finite size, plants grow continuously. / All growth in animals happens by cell division, whereas in plants growth in height is mainly due to cell elongation. / Plant cell division is restricted to areas called meristems, animal cell division takes place throughout the body. / Plant cells retain the ability to differentiate, but most animal cells lose it at an early stage.

Q3 a) Embryonic stem cells can differentiate into any type of body cell. Adult stem cells are less versatile — they can only turn into certain types of cell.

b) E.g. they could be used to grow nerve cells to cure brain damage and spinal injuries / they could be used to grow skin cells for skin grafts.

Q4 a) E.g. stem cell research may lead to cures for a wide variety of diseases

b) E.g. stem cells shouldn't be taken from embryos because each embryo is a potential human life.

Page 63 — Growth

Q1 a) i) E.g. It's easy to measure.

ii) E.g. It's easy to measure.

iii) E.g. It's not affected by the amount of water in the batpig or how much the batpig has recently eaten.

b) i) E.g. It doesn't tell you about changes in width, diameter, etc.

ii) E.g. It's very changeable. The batpig will be heavier if it's just eaten or got a full bladder.

iii) E.g. You'd have to kill the batpig to work it out.

c) dry mass

Q2 a) Growth is steady throughout. / Height increases steadily throughout.

b) i) adolescence

ii) infancy / just after birth

Q3 E.g. When a baby is developing in the womb, the brain grows at a faster rate than the rest of the body. This is because a large and well-developed brain gives humans a big survival advantage.

Pages 64-65 — Respiration

Q1 a) $C_6H_{12}O_6 + 6O_2 \rightarrow 6CO_2 + 6H_2O$ (+ energy)

b) i) make, ATP

ii) energy

c) Respiration is controlled by enzymes and the rate of an enzyme-controlled reaction is affected by temperature and pH.

Q2 a) E.g. Anaerobic respiration releases much less energy per glucose molecule than aerobic respiration. / Anaerobic respiration produces lactic acid, which builds up in the muscles causing pain and fatigue.

b) E.g. If they do not have enough oxygen to meet their energy demand by aerobic respiration. / If they are exercising vigorously.

c) glucose $\rightarrow$ lactic acid (+ energy)

Q3 a) $31.8 \div 26.5 = \mathbf{1.20}$

b) $26.2 \div 29.1 = \mathbf{0.90}$

Q4 a) i) It rises rapidly, then levels off halfway through the race. After the race it drops again.

ii) It follows the same pattern.

iii) his metabolic rate

b) lactic acid

c) Because he has an oxygen debt after the race. Extra oxygen is needed to break down the lactic acid produced by anaerobic respiration during the race, so he needs to keep breathing hard.

d) The lactic acid has to be carried to the liver to be broken down, so his heart rate needs to stay high.

Page 66 — Functions of the Blood

Q1 a) the liquid part of the blood

b) glucose

c) i) E.g. carbon dioxide / urea

ii) E.g. (carbon dioxide) from the body cells to the lungs / (urea) from the liver to the kidneys

d) E.g. hormones / antibodies / water / red and white blood cells / platelets

Q2 biconcave, large, nucleus, haemoglobin, oxygen, oxyhaemoglobin, body tissues, oxygen, capillaries

Page 67 — Blood Vessels

Q1 vein — vessel that takes blood to the heart
valve — keeps the blood flowing in the right direction
artery — vessel that takes blood away from the heart
lumen — hole in the middle of a tube
capillary — vessel involved in the exchange of materials at the tissues

Module B3 — Living and Growing

Q2 a) Veins
b) Capillaries
c) Arteries
d) arteries, veins
Q3 a) i) Blood vessel B because it has thinner walls than blood vessel A but has a wider lumen.
ii) You could look for the presence of valves.
b) Blood vessel A. It has thicker walls and a narrower lumen than blood vessel B, so it must be the artery. Arteries have elastic walls.

Page 68 — The Heart

Q1 a) pulmonary artery
b) vena cava
c) right atrium
d) tricuspid valve
e) right ventricle
f) aorta
g) pulmonary vein
h) semilunar valve
i) bicuspid valve
j) left ventricle
Q2 a) A circulatory system made up of two circuits — one goes to the lungs, the other to the body.
b) Returning blood to the heart after it's picked up oxygen at the lungs means it can be pumped out around the body at a higher pressure. This increases the rate of blood flow to the tissue, so more oxygen can be delivered to the cells.
Q3 a) they prevent the back flow of blood.
b) to pump blood out of the heart
c) The right ventricle only has to pump blood to the lungs, so it doesn't need as much muscle. The left ventricle has to pump blood to the rest of the body, so it needs to be more muscular.

Page 69 — Selective Breeding

Q1 a) It's when humans artificially select the plants or animals that are going to breed, according to what we want from them.
b) Fruit plant: e.g. any two from: larger fruit / sweeter/better tasting fruit / fruit with better colour, fruit that ripens more quickly / more resistant to disease / faster growth rate.
Ornamental house plant: e.g. any two from: more colourful leaves/flowers / better scented flowers / more resistant to disease / faster growth rate.
Q2 E.g. Selective breeding reduces the gene pool/creates inbreeding, which increases the chance of organisms developing genetic disorders. / Selective breeding reduces genetic variation so there's less chance of any resistant alleles being present in the population if a new disease appears
Q3 a) Individuals with more friendly/less aggressive temperament are selected and are bred from — they produce offspring. The most friendly animals are selected again. This process continues over many generations.
b) Selective breeding reduces the gene pool; this means that harmful recessive alleles are more likely to come together to produce a genetic disorder.

Page 70 — Genetic Engineering

Q1 a) 1. The gene for the characteristic is selected.
2. The gene is cut from the DNA and isolated.
3. The gene is inserted into the DNA of another organism.
4. The organism replicates.
b) i) E.g. Organisms with new and useful features can be produced very quickly.

ii) E.g. The inserted gene might have unexpected harmful effects.
c) E.g. Bacteria can be genetically engineered to produce human insulin.
Q2 a) The gene that controls the production of beta-carotene in carrot plants can be put into rice plants. Humans who eat the rice can change the beta-carotene into Vitamin A.
b) E.g. genes could be added that make plants resistant to herbicides, frost damage and disease.
Q3 a) E.g. some people think its wrong to genetically alter organisms purely for human benefit, particularly if the organism that is engineered suffers as a result. / Some people are worried that we'll start genetically engineering human beings. / The impact on future generations is unknown.
b) E.g. Yes — because it can help people (e.g. it can help people with diseases like diabetes, it can help to grow more food, etc.)
OR: No — there could be consequences that nobody has thought of yet.

Page 71 — Gene Therapy and Cloning Animals

Q1 a) Clones are genetically identical organisms.
b) nuclear transfer
c) A. A nucleus is removed from a sheep's egg cell.
B. A nucleus from an udder cell of a different sheep is inserted into the egg cell.
C. The egg cell is given an electric shock to make it start dividing.
D. The embryo is implanted in the uterus of a surrogate mother sheep.
Q2 a) Gene therapy involves altering a person's genes in an attempt to cure genetic disorders.
b) Gene therapy can be used to alter the genes of gametes or body cells.
c) E.g. It might have unexpected consequences which could cause a whole new set of problems. These problems would then be inherited by all future generations. / There are fears that this kind of gene therapy could lead to the creation of 'designer babies' — where parents are able to choose the genes they want their children to have.

Page 72 — Uses and Risks of Cloning Animals

Q1 a) Once the animals have been genetically engineered to have suitable organs, they could be cloned to increase the number of organs available for transplantation.
b) E.g. any two from: Cloned animals might not be as healthy as normal ones. / Cloning might have consequences we're not yet aware of.
c) E.g. Animals like sheep and cows that can produce medicines in their milk (such as the blood clotting agent factor VIII) could be developed by genetic engineering and then cloned.
Q2 The cloned embryos could be used to supply stem cells for stem cell therapy.
Q3 E.g. There would have to be lots of surrogate pregnancies, probably with high rates of miscarriage and stillbirth. / Clones of other mammals have been unhealthy and often die prematurely — which means human clones might too. / Even if a healthy clone were produced, it might be psychologically damaged by the knowledge that it's just a clone of another human being.

Module B4 — It's a Green World

Page 73 — Cloning Plants

Q1 a) 1 — A plant with the desired characteristics is chosen.
2 — Several small pieces of tissue are removed from the parent plant.
3 — The tissue is grown in a growth medium under aseptic conditions.
4 — When the tissues produce shoots and roots they're moved to potting compost to carry on growing.
b) E.g. nutrients / growth hormones.
c) To stop the growth of microbes that could harm the plants.
Q2 Plant cells keep their ability to differentiate whereas animal cells lose this at an early stage.
Q3 a) E.g. You can be fairly sure of the characteristics of the plant because it'll be genetically identical to the parent. / It's possible to mass-produce plants that are hard to grow from seeds.
b) E.g. If the plants suffer from a disease or start doing badly because of a change in environment they'll all have the same problems because they'll all have the same genes. / It will cause a lack of genetic variation.

Pages 74-76 — Mixed Questions — Module B3

Q1 a) Respiration is the process of releasing energy from glucose/food. It happens in every cell.
b) i) oxygen
ii) lactic acid
iii) Less
c) Anaerobic respiration produces lactic acid which builds up in the muscles. When anaerobic respiration stops, the body is left with an oxygen debt because extra oxygen is needed to break down the lactic acid.
Q2 a) i) Cell enlargement is the main method for growth in height in plants, animals don't use this method for growth.
ii) Cell division happens in all parts of animals, in plants cell division usually just happens in areas called meristems (at the tips of roots and shoots).
iii) Most animal cells lose their ability to differentiate at an early stage, plant cells retain this ability.
b) E.g. wet mass is very changeable.
Q3 a) Embryonic stem cells have the ability to differentiate into any type of cell, tissue or organ. Adult stem cells don't.
b) mitosis
c) Embryonic stem cells may eventually be able to grow tissues to treat medical conditions, e.g. nerve cells to cure brain damage and spinal injuries, skin cells for skin grafts, etc.
d) E.g. Some people feel that human embryos shouldn't be used for experiments because each one is a potential human life.
Q4 a) W — pulmonary artery
X — vena cava
Y — pulmonary vein
Z — aorta
b) i) It has strong, elastic walls containing thick layers of muscle to cope with high blood pressure.
ii) It has thin, permeable walls to allow materials to diffuse in and out.
c) i) veins
ii) Valves prevent the backflow of blood.
Q5 a) T–T–A–G–G–T–T–A–G
b) DNA carries a code for making proteins. The base sequence controls which proteins are made. The base sequence determines the sequence of amino acids in the protein. Each amino acid is coded for by 3 bases.
Q6 a) Adult 1, because this adult provided all the genetic material for the clone.
b) i) 54
ii) 27
iii) 54

c) E.g. Animals that could produce medicines in their milk (e.g. factor VIII for treating haemophilia) could be genetically engineered and then cloned. / Animals that have organs suitable for transplantation into humans could be developed by genetic engineering and then cloned. This would ensure a constant supply of organs for transplants.

Module B4 — It's a Green World
Page 77 — Estimating Population Sizes

Q1 a) A population is all the organisms of one species in a habitat. A community is made up of populations of different species.
b) Total area = 250 m x 180 m = 45 000 m²
Total area x number of plants = population
45 000 m² x 11 = 495 000, so there's likely to be approximately **500 000 clover plants**.
c) i) (11 + 9 + 8 + 9 + 7) ÷ 5 = **8.8 plants**
ii) (It is the same field, so use 45 000 m² again.)
45 000 m² x 8.8 = **396 000 clover plants** (≈ 400 000).
d) Lisa's result is likely to be more accurate as she has used a larger sample size.
Q2 a) Population size = (30 × 30) ÷ 7 = 129 ≈ **130**
b) E.g. There are no changes in population size due to deaths, immigration or emigration. / The sampling methods for the capture and recapture are identical. / The marking hasn't affected the individuals' chances of survival.

Page 78 — Ecosystems and Distribution of Organisms

Q1 a) All the organisms living in a particular area, as well as all the non-living (abiotic) conditions.
b) A habitat is just the place where an organism lives, but an ecosystem includes all the organisms and abiotic factors in an area.
c) They contain (almost) everything they need to maintain themselves. The only thing they need from outside the ecosystem is an energy source.
Q2 a) Mark out a line with a tape measure and place quadrats along the line. Count and record the types of moss found in the quadrats.
b) Species 2 was distributed between 0 and 8 m along the transect. It was most common between 2 and 3 m.

Page 79 — Zonation

Q1 a) the non-living, physical factors in an environment
b) E.g. any three from: light / temperature / salinity / water / oxygen / soil quality
Q2 a) It's the gradual change in the distribution of species across a habitat.
b) i) Lichens because they are adapted to survive in zone 4, where there is high light intensity.
ii) E.g. Red seaweed might be better adapted to the low light intensity and low exposure to air in zone 1, allowing it to out-compete the brown seaweed there. The brown seaweed could be better adapted to the higher light intensity and greater exposure to air in zone 2, making it more abundant in zone 2 than zone 1.

Page 80 — Biodiversity

Q1 The number of different species in an area.
The number of different habitats in an area.
The amount of variation between individuals of the same species in an area.

Module B4 — It's a Green World

Q2 a) Natural ecosystems maintain themselves without any major interference from humans. Artificial ecosystems are created and maintained by humans.

b) The lake — it has a greater variety of plant, fish and other animal species than the fish farm.

c) i) E.g. Predator and pest species are removed from fish farms to protect the fish, but are left alone in the lake. / There are more habitats for animals in the lake because there are more plant species. / There's more food in the lake because there are more plant species.

ii) E.g. Fish food in the fish farms can cause algal blooms. These block out the light, killing plants. No food is added to the lake so algal blooms are less likely.

Q3 Forestry plantations have fewer species of tree than natural woodlands because only one tree species is planted at a time. Plantations also have fewer plant species because the densely planted trees leave less room and light for other plants. This results in fewer habitats and fewer animal species than in natural woodland.

Page 81 — Photosynthesis

Q1 $6CO_2 + 6H_2O \rightarrow C_6H_{12}O_6 + 6O_2$

Q2 a) two

b) chloroplasts

c) water

d) carbon dioxide gas

Q3 a) They change stored starch to glucose and use it for respiration to release energy for growth.

b) They use their leaves to make glucose by photosynthesis.

c) E.g. Starch can't dissolve and move away from storage areas in solution. / Starch doesn't affect the water concentration in the cells.

Q4 leaves, energy, convert, cellulose, walls, proteins, lipids.

Page 82 — Understanding Photosynthesis

Q1 They thought that plants must grow and gain mass by taking in minerals from the soil.

Q2 a) The tree was much heavier than at the start of the experiment, but the mass of the soil had changed very little.

b) That the tree must have gained mass by taking in water.

c) His experiment introduced the idea that plants don't just gain mass by taking in minerals from the soil.

Q3 a) It won't be possible to re-light the candle.

b) The candle can now be re-lit.

c) The plant photosynthesised, releasing oxygen into the container and removing carbon dioxide. The presence of oxygen in the container allowed the candle to be re-lit.

Pages 83-84 — More on Photosynthesis

Q1 a) E.g. light intensity, CO_2 concentration, temperature

b) A factor that stops photosynthesis from happening any faster.

Q2 a) b)

Change in conditions	Environmental factor(s) changed	Effect on photosynthesis
A cooling fan is turned on.	temperature	decrease
More plants are added to the room.	carbon dioxide	decrease
Jacquie's family enter the room.	carbon dioxide temperature	increase
An electric heater is switched on.	temperature	increase
A light bulb is switched on.	light	increase
The blinds are closed and lights switched off.	light also accept temperature	decrease

Q3 They supplied photosynthesising plants with normal carbon dioxide (containing oxygen-16) and water containing an isotope of oxygen called oxygen-18. The plants released oxygen-18 during photosynthesis, showing that the oxygen came from the water and not the carbon dioxide.

Q4 a) i) Increasing the air temperatures increases the rate of photosynthesis (up to a point).

ii) More carbon dioxide in the atmosphere increases the rate of photosynthesis, so the plants grow faster.

b) i) after dark / at night

ii) E.g. It provides a high level of light for a longer period allowing photosynthesis to take place for longer.

Q5 a)

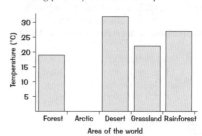

b) Arctic

c) The temperatures are extremely low there, so the rate of photosynthesis will be very low.

Pages 85-86 — Diffusion

Q1 net, higher, lower, random, bigger, large, less

Q2 a)

(The dye molecules will have spread out evenly.)

b) The rate of diffusion would speed up.

c) The dye molecules will move from an area of higher concentration (the dye droplet) to an area of lower concentration (the water).

Q3 a) Switching a fan on will spread the curry particles more quickly through the house.

b) The curry will smell stronger. Adding more curry powder increases the concentration of the curry particles and increases the rate of diffusion of the curry particles to the air.

Q4 a) False

b) False

c) True

d) True

e) False

Q5 B, there is a greater concentration difference between the two sides of the membrane in diagram B so the molecules will diffuse from left to right more quickly.

Q6 a) glucose

b) Starch molecules are too large to fit through the pores in the membrane, but the small glucose molecules would diffuse through to the area of lower glucose concentration outside the bag.

c) Faster, because the surface area of the bag is larger. The more surface there is to move across, the faster the molecules can get from one side to the other.

Module B4 — It's a Green World

Page 87 — Leaves and Diffusion

Q1   A — palisade mesophyll layer
B — upper epidermis
C — waxy cuticle
D — stoma
E — guard cell

Q2 a)   photosynthesis
b)   respiration

Q3 a)   respiration
b)   Respiration releases energy, which plants need to live.
c)   In daylight the plants photosynthesise and take in carbon dioxide.
d)   E.g.

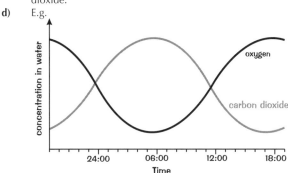

e)   The oxygen concentration falls at night as the plants respire and increases during the day as the plants release oxygen from photosynthesis.

Page 88 — Leaves and Photosynthesis

Q1   air spaces in mesophyll layer — large internal surface area for gas exchange, broad leaves — large surface area exposed to light, guard cells — control when stomata open and close for gas exchange, thin leaves — short diffusion distance

Q2   vascular, xylem, transport, support

Q3   E.g. any three from: chlorophyll a / chlorophyll b / carotene / xanthophyll

Q4 a)   Different pigments absorb different wavelengths of light, so plant cells can make the most of the Sun's energy by absorbing as much of it as possible.
b)   The palisade layer is near the top of the leaf, so this is where the chloroplasts will get the most light.
c)   Allows light to pass through it to the palisade layer where most of the chloroplasts are.

Pages 89-90 — Osmosis

Q1   water, partially, membrane, higher, lower, diffusion, random

Q2 a)   B
b)   A membrane with tiny holes in it. The holes allow small molecules (like water) to pass through, but not larger ones.
c)   The liquid level on side B will fall, because there is a net flow of water molecules away from side B to side A.

Q3 a)   Water will move into the red blood cell because the concentration of water in the cell is lower than in the plasma.
b) i)   If an animal cells takes in too much water it will burst — lysis.
ii)   If an animal cell loses too much water it shrivels up — crenation.

Q4 a)

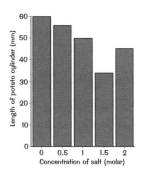

b)

Concentration of salt solution (molar)	Final length of potato cylinder (mm)	Change in length of potato cylinder (mm)
0.0	60	+10
0.5	56	+6
1.0	50	0
1.5	34	-16
2.0	45	-5

c) i)   1.5 molar
ii)   E.g. Repeat the experiment at least twice and take the averages.
d)   E.g. any three from: the volume of solution / the length of time the cylinders are left for / the surface area of the cylinders / the temperature

Q5 a)   A — normal
B — turgid
C — flaccid
D — plasmolysed
b)   The cells lose water and their contents are no longer able to push up against the inelastic cell wall. Turgor pressure is lost, so the leaf goes limp.
c)   The inelastic cell wall keeps everything in position.

Page 91 — Transport Systems in Plants

Q1

Xylem vessels	Phloem vessels
transport water transport substances up the stem made of dead cells	made of living cells transport substances both up and down the stem transport food

Q2 a)

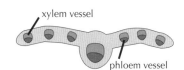

b)

vascular bundle

Q3 a)   A = phloem, B = xylem
b)   To transport food (sugars) made in the leaves to the rest of the plant.
c)   E.g. It might have root hairs around the outside. / The xylem would be in the centre with the phloem arranged around it. / The xylem and phloem are central (not arranged as vascular bundles around the outside).

Module B4 — It's a Green World

Q4 a) minerals, water

b) They have thick cellulose side walls and are made of lots of dead cells joined end to end with a hole (lumen) down the middle.

Pages 92-93 — Water Flow Through Plants

Q1 a) b) c) E.g.

Q2 a)

b) Water moves from an area of higher concentration in the soil, to an area of lower concentration in the cell by osmosis.

Q3 E.g. It helps to keep the plant cool / the plant has a constant supply of water for photosynthesis / it creates a turgor pressure which provides support / essential minerals from the soil are brought into the plant with the water.

Q4 leaves, evaporation/diffusion, diffusion/evaporation, stem, xylem, roots, transpiration, photosynthesis

Q5 a) False

b) True

c) True

d) False

Q6 Increasing the temperature increases the transpiration rate. When it's warm, the water molecules have more energy to evaporate and diffuse out of the stomata.

Q7 a) E.g. stomata are mostly found on the lower surface of the leaf where it's cool and dark. There is a waterproof waxy cuticle covering the leaf surface.

b) They have no stomata on the upper epidermis and fewer, smaller ones on the underside of the leaf.

Q8 a)

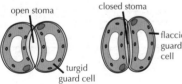

open stoma   closed stoma

turgid guard cell

flaccid guard cell

b) i) turgid

ii) flaccid

iii) close, low

c) Open, because the plant will be using the sunlight to photosynthesise and so it needs to take in CO_2.

Pages 94-95 — Minerals Needed for Healthy Growth

Q1 Magnesium — for making chlorophyll
Nitrates — for making amino acids and proteins
Phosphates — for making DNA and cell membranes
Potassium — for helping enzymes to function

Q2 a) There aren't enough nitrates in the soil.

b) Poultry manure because it has the highest nitrate content.

Q3 a) As controls — to allow a comparison between them and the plants that were grown in solutions deficient in one mineral.

b) i) Plants will have poor root growth and discoloured leaves.

ii) The leaves of the plants will be yellow.

c) To show that any symptoms were definitely caused by the deficiency of a certain mineral. If other minerals had also been deficient, you wouldn't know which mineral deficiency caused the symptoms.

Q4 a) The magnesium levels gradually decreased from 2000 to 2010.

b) Magnesium is required to make chlorophyll, which is needed for photosynthesis.

c) Plants deficient in magnesium have yellow leaves.

Q5 a) root hair cell

b) Absorbing water and minerals from the soil.

c) It has a very large surface area for absorbing the minerals and water.

d) The soil generally has a lower concentration of minerals than the root hair cells. (Diffusion only takes place from areas of higher concentration to areas of lower concentration.)

e) Active transport uses energy from respiration to move mineral ions from the soil into the root against the concentration gradient.

Page 96 — Decay

Q1 detritivores, woodlice, detritus, surface area, saprophytes, extracellular

Q2 a) E.g.

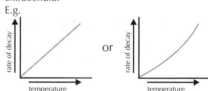

rate of decay   or   rate of decay

temperature   temperature

b) The warmer the temperature the faster the microbes will respire and reproduce and therefore the quicker things will decay.

c)

Conditions	Rank
Dry, cold, no oxygen	3
Moist, warm, oxygen	1
Moist, cold, no oxygen	2

Q3 Canning — keeps decomposers out.
Freezing — decomposers can't reproduce at such low temperatures.
Pickling — the acidic conditions kill any decomposers.
Drying — decomposers need water, so can't survive.

Q4 The salt solution will cause decomposers to lose water by osmosis, drying them out and killing them.

Page 97 — Intensive Farming

Q1 Using herbicides — kills weeds — more energy from the Sun is used by the crops
Using insecticides — kills insects — less energy is transferred to another food chain
Battery farming — animals kept in small pens — less energy wasted on movement and keeping warm

Q2 a) hydroponics

b) A mixture of fertilisers dissolved in water / a nutrient solution.

c) E.g. tomatoes

d) i) Disadvantage

ii) Disadvantage

iii) Advantage

iv) Advantage

Module B5 — The Living Body

Q3 a) E.g. Some people think it is cruel / unethical to keep animals cramped in tiny cages.

b) E.g. Careless use of fertilisers can pollute rivers and lakes (known as eutrophication). / Removal of hedges to make larger fields destroys the natural habitat of wild creatures. / Pesticides disturb food chains.

Page 98 — Pesticides and Biological Control

Q1 E.g. they may kill organisms that aren't pests / they're persistent, so they can be passed along (and accumulate in) food chains.

Q2 The frog population would decrease as there's less for them to eat, so the foxes would have to eat more rabbits. The populations of both rabbits and foxes could therefore decrease too.

Q3 a) Biological control is when living organisms rather than chemicals are used to control a pest species.

b) Advantages: E.g. any two from: no chemicals are used / there's less pollution / there's less disruption of food chains / there's less risk to people eating the food.
Disadvantages: E.g. any two from: the predator might not eat the pest / the predator might eat useful species / the predator species might get out of control / the predator might not stay in the area where it's needed.

Q4 a) The birds of prey ate animals that had eaten the crops.

b) Each small animal ate a lot of crops, and each bird ate a lot of the small animals. If the chemical was not excreted it would build up through the food chain and reach toxic levels.

Page 99 — Alternatives to Intensive Farming

Q1 a) Using insecticides: Alternatives include biological control / crop rotation / varying seed planting times. Advantage: No chemicals used so safer for humans eating the crops / less likely to disrupt food chains / doesn't kill harmless or beneficial organisms.

b) Using herbicides: Alternatives include weeding. Advantage: No chemicals used (see above).

c) Using chemical fertilisers: Alternatives include manure/ compost / crop rotation. Advantage: No chemicals used (see above). Less chance of polluting rivers (causing eutrophication).

Q2 a) Sowing seeds later or earlier in the season will avoid the major pests, meaning that the farmer won't need to use pesticides.

b) Growing a cycle of different crops in a field each year stops the pests and diseases of one crop building up. It also stops nutrients running out (as each crop has slightly different needs).

Q3 drawbacks, space, wildlife, workers, expensive, less

Pages 100-102 — Mixed Questions — Module B4

Q1 a) He uses pesticides to kill pests that damage his crops.

b) Pesticides tend to also be toxic to creatures that aren't pests. The concentration of pesticide can increase up a food chain, which could result in a lethal dose for the buzzards.

c) They stay around in ecosystems for a long time and are hard to get rid of.

d) i) magnesium, potassium
ii) nitrate
iii) poor flower and fruit growth and discoloured leaves

Q2 a)

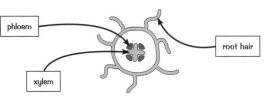

b) lower, diffusion, active transport, respiration

Q3 a) Osmosis is the net movement of water molecules across a partially permeable membrane from a region of higher water concentration (i.e. a dilute solution) to a region of lower water concentration (i.e. a concentrated solution).

b) i) A
ii) C
iii) B

c) i)

Treatment	Line
kept in normal conditions	C
covered, clear plastic bag	D
fanned, cool air	B
fanned, warm air	A
covered, black plastic bag	E

ii) If the air is humid, there's not much difference in the water concentration between the inside and the outside of the leaf. As a result, water diffuses out of the leaf very slowly and the transpiration rate is low.

Q4 a) Nitrogen-fixing crops help to put nitrates back into the soil.

b) Plants need nitrogen to make proteins for cell growth. If they don't have enough, the plants will be stunted and their older leaves will be yellow.

Q5 a) Increasing the concentration of carbon dioxide increases the rate of photosynthesis (up to a certain point).

b) temperature

c) The rate of photosynthesis does not continue to increase because temperature or the levels of carbon dioxide act as limiting factors.

d) E.g. any three from: they're broad / they're thin / they contain air spaces in the spongy mesophyll layer / they have guard cells and stomata.

Module B5 — The Living Body
Page 103 — Bones and Cartilage

Q1 E.g. any three from: It gives the body support and provides a framework. / It's easy to attach muscles to it. / It's more flexible than an external skeleton. / It can easily grow with the body.

Q2 a) A — head, B — shaft, C — marrow cavity / bone marrow
b) a layer of cartilage
c) They're lighter and stronger than solid bones of the same size and mass, which makes movement far more efficient.

Q3 grow, repair, infected, broken, knock, calcium/phosphorus, phosphorus/calcium, ossification, cartilage

Q4 a) They often suffer from osteoporosis, which makes the bones softer, more brittle and more likely to break.

b) If you move someone with a fracture the bone may injure nearby tissue.

Page 104 — Joints and Muscles

Q1 hinge, one, ball, socket, rotate

Q2 Cartilage — Acts as a shock absorber
Synovial membrane — Produces synovial fluid
Ligaments — Hold the bones together
Synovial fluid — Lubricates the joint

Module B5 — The Living Body

Q3 a) A - biceps, B - triceps
b) elbow
c) A
d) B
e) The triceps contracts and the biceps relaxes.

Pages 105-106 — Circulatory Systems

Q1 oxygen, glucose, waste, diffusion, large, slow, circulatory
Q2 a) away from, high
b) towards, low
Q3 a) It decreases.
b) A - arteries, B - capillaries, C - veins
Q4 a) fish — single circulatory system — one circuit of blood vessels from the heart
mammals — double circulatory system — two circuits of blood vessels from the heart
b) i) One chamber is needed to receive blood and the other is needed to pump blood out to the body.
ii) Two chambers are needed so that blood can be pumped to the lungs and the rest of the body separately. The other two chambers are needed so that blood can be received separately from the lungs and the body.
Q5 a) true
b) true
c) false
d) false
Q6 a) In a single circulatory system the blood loses pressure as it's pumped to the gills and around the body. In a double circulatory system blood loses pressure in the lungs, but returns to the heart before being pumped to the rest of the body. This increases the pressure of the blood going to the body.
b) E.g. Materials can be transported around the body more quickly.

Page 107 — The Cardiac Cycle and Circulation

Q1 2. The atria contract, pushing blood into the ventricles.
3. The ventricles contract.
4. Blood flows into the pulmonary artery and aorta.
5. The cycle starts again as blood flows into the atria.
Q2 a) Semilunar valves closed, Atrio-ventricular valves open
b) Semilunar valves open, Atrio-ventricular valves closed
c) Semilunar valves closed, Atrio-ventricular valves open
Q3 a) E.g. any two from: What the heart valves do. / The heart is a pump (rather than something that sucks). / The same blood is circulated around the body over and over again — not manufactured and consumed. / The pulse is caused by the heart pumping blood into the arteries.
b) Claudius Galen thought that blood was produced in the heart and in the liver and consumed by the organs.

Pages 108-109 — Heart Rate

Q1 a) i) B
ii) D
b) E.g. it delivers more oxygenated blood to the muscles.
c) adrenaline
Q2 electric current, SAN, muscle, atria, contract, AVN, electric current, muscle, ventricles, contract, atria, ventricles, electric current, skin, wire
Q3 a) The electrical activity of the heart.
b) A - atria contract, B - ventricles contract, C - ventricles relax, D - one heartbeat / cardiac cycle
c) A fast heartbeat.
d) E.g. heart attacks / an irregular heartbeat

Q4 a) An ultrasound scan of the heart.
b) E.g. an enlarged heart / decreased pumping ability / poor valve function

Page 110 — Heart Disease

Q1 a) Valve damage — blood doesn't circulate as effectively as normal — replacement by artificial valves
Coronary heart disease — reduces blood flow to the heart muscle — coronary bypass surgery
b) A piece of blood vessel from another part of the body is used to bypass the blockage in the heart blood vessel.
c) E.g. When a patient with a failing heart is waiting for a heart transplant.
Q2 a) i) A gap in the wall separating the two ventricles or the two atria.
ii) It allows blood to move directly from one side of the heart to the other.
b) Oxygenated blood and deoxygenated blood mix, and this reduces the amount of oxygen that gets pumped to the body.
c) surgery
Q3 a) E.g. Rejection isn't normally a problem. / They're much less drastic procedures than a transplant.
b) E.g. The new valves and pacemakers might not last very long and need replacing as a result.

Pages 111-112 — Blood Clotting and Transfusions

Q1 a) A mesh of protein/fibrin fibres.
b) Clots are formed by a series of chemical reactions that take place when platelets in your blood are exposed to damaged blood vessels.
Q2 warfarin/heparin/aspirin (in any order), prevent, haemophilia, inherited
Q3 a) A, B, AB, O
b) A substance that can trigger an immune reaction.
c) blood clumping together
d) In the plasma
Q4

Blood group	Antigens present	Antibodies present
A	A	anti-B
B	B	anti-A
AB	A, B	none
O	none	anti-A, anti-B

Q5 a) E.g. During surgery / after an accident / when you've lost lots of blood.
b) i) no
ii) yes
iii) yes
iv) no
c) O
d) O
e) Group A blood contains anti-B antibodies. If it came into contact with group B antigens it would cause agglutination (blood clumping).
Q6 To prevent the blood from clotting.

Page 113 — Transplants and Organ Donation

Q1 a) i) E.g. kidney / part of the liver
ii) E.g. any two from: relatively young / a similar body weight to the patient / a close tissue match to the patient (usually a close family member) / over 18

Module B5 — The Living Body

b) E.g. They must be relatively young, a similar body weight to the patient and a close tissue match. They must also have died very recently and close relatives must give their permission for their organ to be used.

Q2 surgery, success, organ, age, skill, rejection, drugs

Q3 a)

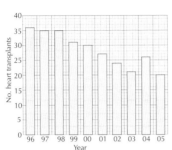

b) The number of heart transplants has generally decreased from 1996 to 2005.

c) i) E.g. more surgeons may learn how to do the operation. / There may be more hearts available for transplant.

ii) E.g. Alternative (less risky) procedures may be developed.

Page 114 — Organ Donation and Organ Replacement

Q1 a) There's a shortage of people willing to be donors. Not all donated organs will be the right tissue match for the patient who needs them. Donors must be roughly the same size and age as the patient who needs their organs.

b) i) E.g. It makes it easier for someone to donate their organs after they've died.

ii) E.g. Doctors may still need the consent of the donor's family to use the donor's organs.

Q2 a) E.g. heart-lung machine / ventilator / kidney dialysis machine

b) E.g. They usually need a constant power supply. / They're often large and difficult to move around. / They must be made from materials that won't harm the body and won't degrade (i.e. break down or rust). / Even if they're made from the right materials, they can occasionally cause inflammation or allergic reactions in the body.

Page 115 — The Respiratory System

Q1 a) toxic, high
b) brain, increasing

Q2

Inspiration	Expiration
Intercostal muscles and diaphragm contract	Diaphragm and intercostal muscles relax
Thorax volume increases	Thorax volume decreases
Pressure in lungs decreases	Pressure in lungs increases
Air enters the lungs	Air is pushed out of the lungs

Q3 a) a spirometer
b) tidal air
c) Total lung capacity minus residual air. / The maximum volume of air that can be breathed in or out.

d) i) ii)

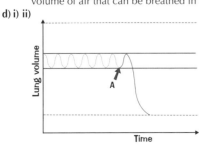

Page 116 — More on the Respiratory System

Q1 a) i) B
ii) D
iii) A
iv) C
b) diffusion

Q2 E.g. A large surface area to increase the rate of diffusion. / A moist surface to help oxygen and carbon dioxide dissolve. / A thin lining so gases don't have to diffuse very far. / A good blood supply. / A permeable surface to help gases exchange easily.

Q3 a) i) Through the lungs and the skin.
ii) Their skins needs to be kept moist to help gaseous exchange through the skin. This means they have to live in moist environments. They can't live in dry environments as their skin is not waterproof, so they would lose too much water.

b) i) fish, gills, filaments
ii) Water supports the gills by keeping the gill filaments separated from one another. Taken out of water the gill filaments stick together and the fish suffocates.

Page 117 — Lung Disease

Q1 a) i) Catches dirt and microbes before they reach the lungs.
ii) Catch dirt and microbes and to push mucus out of the lungs as phlegm.
b) E.g. trachea, bronchi
c) The lungs are a dead end so microbes can't be flushed out.

Q2 a) Cystic fibrosis is inherited/genetic. A thick, sticky mucus is produced which can clog up the bronchioles. This makes breathing difficult and can lead to infection.
b) Asbestosis is caused by breathing in asbestos, usually in an industrial setting. It can cause inflammation and scarring, which limits gas exchange.
c) Lung cancer can be caused by lifestyle, e.g. smoking. Cells divide out of control, forming tumours that reduce the surface area in the lungs.

Q3 lining, inflamed, muscles, contract, difficult, a tight chest/wheezing, wheezing/a tight chest, inhaler

Page 118 — Digestion

Q1 Large insoluble molecules in food need to be broken down into small food molecules, so they can pass more easily into your blood plasma or lymph.

Q2 E.g.

	Active in...	Also active in...
Carbohydrases	the small intestine	the mouth
Proteases	the small intestine	the stomach
Lipases	the small intestine	

Q3
protease
↓
a) protein → amino acids

lipase
↓
b) fat → glycerol + fatty acids

carbohydrase enzymes
↓   ↓
c) starch → maltose → glucose

Q4 It allows food to pass easily through the digestive system and provides a larger surface area for chemical digestion.

Module B5 — The Living Body

Page 119 — More on Digestion

Q1 acidic, protease, small intestine, alkaline

Q2 gall bladder, neutralises, enzymes, fat, emulsification, lipase

Q3 The products of carbohydrate and protein digestion diffuse directly from the intestines to the blood plasma.
The products of fat digestion diffuse out of the gut into the lymphatic system. From there, they're emptied into the blood.

Q4 E.g. any two from: It's very long, so there's time to break down and absorb the food before it reaches the end. / There's a big surface area for absorption because the walls are covered in millions of tiny projections called villi. / Each cell on the surface of a villus also has its own microvilli to increase the surface area even more. / Villi have a single permeable layer of surface cells and a very good blood supply to allow quick absorption.

Page 120 — The Kidneys

Q1 a) cortex
b) medulla
c) renal artery
d) ureter
Q2 a) i) in the liver
ii) excess amino acids
b) They filter substances out of the blood under high pressure and then reabsorb the useful things.
c) urine
Q3 urea, capsule, glomerulus/capsule, capsule/glomerulus, nephron, selectively, ADH, salt, selectively

Pages 121-122 — Waste Removal

Q1 a) negative feedback
b)

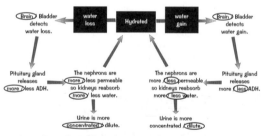

Q2 a) E.g. any three from: how hot it is / the amount of exercise taken / water intake / amount of ADH in the blood.
b) i) more concentrated
ii) more concentrated
iii) large
iv) dilute
v) more concentrated
c) When you exercise you get hot and sweat. Water is lost in the sweat so the kidneys reabsorb more water and therefore produce more concentrated urine.
Q3 E.g. It prevents too much water moving into or out of the tissue by osmosis. / It keeps the blood pressure constant.
Q4 a) Excess sodium, Urea
b)

c) i) It has the same concentration of sodium and glucose as normal blood plasma.
ii) So that glucose and normal levels of sodium are not removed from the plasma.

Page 123 — The Menstrual Cycle

Q1 a)

Effect	FSH	LH	Progesterone	Oestrogen
Causes the lining of the uterus to repair (thicken and grow)				✔
Causes egg to develop in ovaries	✔			
Controls ovulation		✔		
Maintains uterus lining			✔	

b) FSH, LH
c) i) follicle-stimulating hormone
ii) luteinising hormone
Q2 a) negative feedback
b) Progesterone inhibits the release of — LH.
Oestrogen inhibits the release of — FSH.
LH indirectly stimulates the production of — progesterone.
FSH stimulates the ovaries to produce — oestrogen.

Pages 124-125 — Controlling Fertility

Q1 a) i) True
ii) False
iii) False
iv) True
v) True
b) E.g. For artificial insemination to be successful the couple do not need to have sex.
If a woman has low levels of FSH she would be given an injection of FSH.
Q2 Oestrogen is taken every day to keep the level of it permanently high. This mimics pregnancy and inhibits the release of FSH. After a while egg development and production stop.
Q3 a) amniocentesis, needle, fluid, chromosomes, Down's Syndrome
b) E.g. If the foetus has a genetic defect, the parents may consider whether or not to continue the pregnancy. / Foetal screening like amniocentesis can increase the risk of miscarriage.
Q4 a) A woman's eggs are fertilised outside of the body.
b) E.g. the sperm / eggs / uterus.
c) to stimulate egg production
d) A woman who has fertilised eggs — of whom she is not the biological parent — implanted into her uterus. She carries the baby through pregnancy and gives birth. A surrogate mother would be used if the biological mother has an unhealthy uterus or is prone to miscarriage.
e) The chances of multiple pregnancies are increased, which can be a danger to the mother's health.
f) i) E.g they are thrown away / they can be donated to medical research.
ii) E.g. they see this as morally wrong because it is denying the embryo the chance of life.
g) E.g. They can give an infertile couple a child.

Pages 126-127 — More on Growth

Q1 a) pituitary gland
b) growth, long bones
Q2 genes, hormone imbalance
Q3 Exercise builds muscles, and weight-bearing exercise can increase bone mass. Exercise also stimulates the release of growth hormone.
Q4 No, although the baby's growth has slowed down its mass is still above the 2nd percentile for its age.

21121

Module B6 — Beyond the Microscope

Q5 a) People are financially better off — Healthier diet and lifestyle
Medical advances — Previously fatal conditions can now be treated
Improved working and housing conditions — Safer and healthier environment

b) E.g. Any two from: shortage of housing / increased environmental pollution / the state's inability to provide pensions and medical care.

Q6 a) false
b) false
c) true

Q7 a)

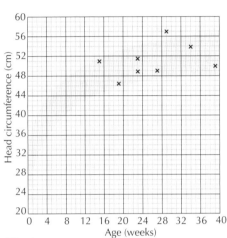

b) Oliver's
c) To provide an early warning of any growth problems.

Pages 128-131 — Mixed Questions — Module B5

Q1 a) A ball and socket joint.
b) The joint can move in all directions and can also rotate.
c) ligaments
d) B and O.

Q2 a) It increases when you exercise and decreases back to normal when you stop.
b) the pacemaker cells / AVN and SAN
c) When you exercise you sweat to keep cool. This means that water is lost from the body. So the amount of urine is decreased to keep water levels in the body constant.
d) ADH (anti-diuretic hormone)

Q3 a) E.g. Artificial insemination / FSH injections / in vitro fertilisation
b) E.g. There could be an 'opt-out' system where anyone's organs can be used unless the person has registered to say that they don't want them to be donated.

Q4 a) Removal of urea from the blood / adjustment of salt levels / adjustment of water content.
b) i) 5.1 g
ii) There is less sweating so the blood is more dilute, excess water is lost in urine.
c) E.g. The organ might be rejected by the patient's immune system. / The patient will have to take immuno-suppressive drugs that leave them more vulnerable to infection.

d)

Blood Group	Can give blood to	Can get blood from
A	A and AB	A and O
B	B and AB	B and O
AB	only AB	anyone
O	anyone	only O

Q5 a) It reduces blood flow to the heart muscle and can result in a heart attack.
b) E.g. ECG / echocardiogram
c) Can cause lung cancer.
d) i) G
ii) H
iii) D
iv) E
e) E.g. any two from: Some people think for religious reasons that a person's body should be buried intact (so giving organs is wrong). / Some people think that life or death is up to God (so receiving organs is wrong). / Some people worry that doctors might not save them if they're critically ill and their organs are needed for transplant. / There are worries that people may get pressured into being a 'living donor' (e.g. donating a kidney to a close relative).

Q6 a) Any two from: Causes the lining of the uterus to repair (thicken and grow). / Stimulates the production of LH. / Inhibits the production of FSH.
b) Her eggs won't develop properly.

Q7 E, B, D, C, A

Q8 a) They are made of living cells.
b) Blood vessels deposit calcium and phosphorus in the cartilage which eventually turns it into bone.
c) length / mass / head circumference
d) A poor diet, particularly if it's low in proteins (needed to make new cells) or minerals (for bone growth), may mean that a child doesn't grow as much as its genes would allow.

Module B6 — Beyond the Microscope

Pages 132-133 — Bacteria

Q1 a) DNA — controls the cell's activities and replication
Flagellum — helps the cell to move
Cell wall — maintains the cell's shape and helps to stop the cell from bursting
b) Small loops of DNA found in the cytoplasm.

Q2 spheres, fission, asexual, two, warm

Q3 a) E.g. any three from: soil / water / air / the human body / food
b) They can consume a wide range of organic nutrients to get energy. Some can even produce their own nutrients.

Q4 sterilised, pasteurised, *Lactobacillus*, incubated, lactic acid, flavours, packaged

Q5 a) Bacteria reproduce more rapidly when they are warm. If food is stored in a fridge, the cold temperature slows down the bacteria's reproduction rate and so the food won't go off as quickly.
b) They can reproduce and cause disease before the body has a chance to respond.

Q6 a) E.g. to avoid contaminating his sample / to protect himself from infection
b) E.g. he should wear gloves and sterilise all his equipment before and after use. He should also seal the dish once he's transferred the bacteria onto it and dispose of the culture safely once he's finished with it.

Module B6 — Beyond the Microscope

Page 134 — Microorganisms and Disease

Q1 a) i) protein coat
ii) genetic material
b) i) true
ii) true
iii) false
c) i) The virus attaches itself to a specific host cell and injects its genetic material into the cell.
ii) The virus uses the host cell to make the components of new viruses.
iii) The host cell splits open — releasing the new viruses.
Q2 Influenza — Airborne droplets — e.g. sneezing into a tissue / washing your hands properly / disinfecting contaminated surfaces
Cholera — Water — e.g. good sanitation
Food poisoning — Food — e.g. good hygiene / making sure food is properly cooked before it's eaten
Q3 E.g. developing countries are poorer than developed countries and so are less likely to be able to afford good sanitation and public health measures. There could be a lack of clean water or an ineffective sewage system, both of which can lead to cholera infections spreading.

Page 135 — Treating Infectious Diseases

Q1 a) viruses
b) Both are used to kill bacteria or stop them growing.
c) Antiseptics are used outside the body whereas antibiotics are used inside the body. / Antiseptics are used to prevent infection rather than antibiotics which are used to treat existing infections.
Q2 Once a microbe has entered the body it reproduces rapidly. The microorganisms begin to produce toxins which damage the cells and tissues. The toxins lead to symptoms of the disease developing and the immune system's reaction can lead to more symptoms such as swelling or fever.
Q3 a) 1. Random mutations in bacterial DNA can lead to it being less affected by a particular antibiotic.
2. Bacteria with these mutated genes are more likely to survive and reproduce in a host being treated with the antibiotic.
3. The gene for antibiotic resistance will be passed on to lots of offspring.
4. The gene becomes more common in the population over time — giving the population resistance to the antibiotic.
b) i) Using antibiotics creates a situation where resistant bacteria have an advantage and increase in numbers — so using antibiotics less will make it less likely that antibiotic resistance will spread.
ii) Failing to complete a course of antibiotics can increase the risk of antibiotic resistance emerging.

Page 136 — More on Infectious Diseases

Q1 a) Can lead to contamination of drinking water with disease-causing microorganisms.
b) Food can't be stored safely and may spoil rapidly.
c) They might move to temporary camps with large numbers of people living in unsanitary conditions where diseases could easily be spread.
Q2 a) False
b) True
c) True
d) False
e) False
Q3 a) In Flask 1, because microbes entered the flask from the air.
b) The microbes settled in the loop of the curved neck, so they did not reach the broth.

c) Flask 1 is the control — it shows that any difference between what happens to the two samples of broth is due to the flask's shape.
d) E.g. Pasteur wanted the flask to be open to the air, to show that it was microbes and not the air itself that caused the broth to spoil.

Page 137 — Yeast

Q1 a) $C_6H_{12}O_6 \rightarrow 2C_2H_5OH + 2CO_2$ (+ energy)
b) glucose $\rightarrow$ ethanol + carbon dioxide (+energy)
c) oxygen, anaerobically, fermentation, oxygen, aerobically
Q2 a) A = Amount of food
B = pH
C = Temperature
D = Amount of toxic waste
b) E.g. Measure how much glucose is broken down over a set period of time.
Q3 a) Because bacteria would feed on the sugar and reproduce rapidly, removing all the oxygen from the water and causing the death of other water life.
b) Yeast will use up the sugar in the water during respiration.

Pages 138-139 — Brewing

Q1 a) 1. Sugar is extracted from barley grains and hops are added.
2. Yeast is added and the mixture is incubated.
3. The beer is drawn off.
4. The beer is pasteurised.
b) Yeast is added to ferment the sugar into alcohol.
c) air, unwanted microorganisms
d) They remove particles from the beer and make it clearer.
Q2 anaerobically, increases, kill, decreases, tolerate, high, high
Q3 a) Fermentation — when anaerobic respiration happens to produce carbon dioxide, ethanol and energy.
b) Distillation — when the fermented liquid is heated to separate the alcohol from the mixture.
c) Pasteurisation — liquids are heated to kill off any micro-organisms present.
Q4 a) The grapes are mashed and water added. Yeast is added and the mixture incubated in a fermenting vessel. The yeast ferments the sugar in the grapes into alcohol. The wine produced is drawn off through a tap and clarifying agents may be added.
b) Beer is pasteurised to kill any remaining yeast and completely stop fermentation. This is because it could otherwise spoil if kept in the wrong conditions. Wine isn't pasteurised because it improves the taste if it is allowed to go on slowly fermenting.
Q5 a) The fermented liquid is heated to 78 °C to boil the alcohol and turn it into a vapour. The alcohol vapour rises, leaving the water behind, and travels through a cooled tube where it condenses back into liquid and runs into a collecting vessel.
b) on licensed premises

Pages 140-141 — Biofuels

Q1 organic, energy, transferred, wood, fermented, bacteria, biogas
Q2 a) Methane and carbon dioxide.
b) E.g. hydrogen, nitrogen, hydrogen sulfide
c) It can be explosive.
Q3 Biogas is burned to heat water — Produces steam to heat central heating systems.
Burned to drive an engine — Powers cars and buses.
Burned to power a turbine — Generates electricity.
Q4 a) Some bacteria decompose the organic matter and produce waste, then another type are needed to decompose that waste, and so on, till you get biogas.

Module B6 — Beyond the Microscope

b) By using a continuous flow method, where organic waste is continuously fed into the digester and biogas and solid digested material are continually removed.

Q5 a) 35 °C

b) E.g. this was the optimum temperature for the bacteria's respiration.

c) E.g. this temperature was too hot and killed the bacteria.

Page 142 — More on Biofuels

Q1 a) i) false

ii) true

iii) false

iv) true

b) E.g. biofuels are an alternative to fossil fuels. Biogas is a 'cleaner' fuel than diesel or petrol.

Q2 rate, hasn't

Q3 E.g. habitat loss / extinction of species

Q4 a) About 10 % ethanol and 90 % petrol.

b) as fuel for cars

c) Brazil

d) E.g. plenty of sugar cane

Page 143 — Soils

Q1 a) i) clay

ii) loam

iii) sand

b) Clay soils have small particles, which pack tightly together leaving small pores. This gives little room for air.

c) decomposed, dead organic matter found in soils

Q2 a) E.g. Take the mass of each soil sample. Heat each soil sample to 105 °C until it reaches a constant mass — this will boil off all the water. Take the mass of each soil sample again and subtract these values from the original values. This will give you the mass of water in each of the original soil samples.

b) Darren's soil / the sandy soil

c) The large particles in the sandy soil create large pores and allow water to drain out of the soil. Water molecules cling to the small particles in clay soils, causing them to retain more water.

Page 144 — Life in the Soil

Q1 a) E.g. there could be an increase in the number of small mites because they eat the same dead organisms as the woodlice.

b) E.g. the number of wire worms may decrease because of increased competition between wire worms and small mites for plant roots.

Q2 Humus releases minerals and nutrients into the soil. It also increases the air content of the soil, making oxygen available to soil organisms.

Q3 Darwin, aeration, oxygen, drainage, neutralise, fertile, layers, nutrients

Page 145 — Life in Water

Q1 Advantages — any two from: plentiful supply of water / less variation in temperature / the water provides support / waste disposal is easier.
Disadvantages — any two from: more energy needed to move through water / effects of osmosis could damage cells so water intake must be carefully regulated.

Q2 The robber crab, because there is more variation in temperature on the land where this crab lives.

Q3 E.g. water provides support for aquatic plants, so there is no need for them to be woody.

Q4 a) E.g. the difference in solute concentration between the Amoeba cell and the surrounding water means that water moves into the Amoeba by osmosis.

b) Water taken up by osmosis is collected in the vacuole which then contracts to empty the water outside the cell.

c) E.g. the solute concentration in the cell is the same as or lower than that outside, so no water enters by osmosis and there's no need to get rid of excess water.

Pages 146-147 — More on Life in Water

Q1 a) fertiliser

b) i) 1. Algae die and decay.
2. Decomposers feed on dead algae.
3. All the oxygen in the water is used up.
4. Animals are unable to respire and die.

ii) eutrophication

Q2 a) In the summer there is more light and a higher temperature, allowing a faster rate of photosynthesis and faster growth.

b) More phytoplankton means there is more food for zooplankton, so the zooplankton increase in numbers.

Q3 E.g. any three from: fertilisers / sewage / DDT / PCBs

Q4 light, seasons, low, temperature, high, lower

Q5 a) bacteria

b) dead, decomposing material that slowly falls to the sea bed

Q6 The levels of bacteria increase downstream from the outflow pipe. The sewage provides extra nutrients causing rapid algal growth. The algae will then die, providing food for bacteria that feed on the dead algae. This causes an increase in the numbers of bacteria.

Q7 a) DDT can't be broken down, so it remains in the bodies of organisms and is passed on to animals higher in the food chain when they feed.

b) Organisms at the top of the food chain (e.g. whales) are more likely to be poisoned. Each organism in a food chain eats several of the organisms below it, so the concentration of the DDT increases at each stage in the food chain.

c) E.g. PCBs

Page 148 — Enzymes in Action

Q1 a) to break down (insoluble) proteins in stains on clothing

b) E.g. amylase, to break down carbohydrates / lipase, to break down fats (lipids)

c) The digestion products are soluble in water, so can be washed out of the clothing easily.

Q2 a) The enzymes in the powder can be denatured by extremes of pH.

b) The enzymes in the powder can be denatured by very high temperatures.

Q3 It's used to change sucrose into glucose and fructose. These sugars are much sweeter than sucrose, so less sugar can be added to food. It's used to make low-calorie food sweeter.

Page 149 — More Enzymes in Action

Q1 a) The enzymes are mixed with alginate gel, which is then dropped into a calcium chloride solution.

b) Immobilised enzymes can be used in continuous flow processes.
Immobilised enzymes don't contaminate the product.

Q2 Immobilised enzymes are used so that the enzymes stay on the strip when dipped in blood.

Q3 a) They can't break down lactose because they don't produce the lactase enzyme.

b) Bacteria in the gut would ferment the lactose, causing abdominal pain, wind and diarrhoea.

c) The milk is run through a column of immobilised lactase enzymes, which break down the lactose in the milk into glucose and galactose. Lactose-free milk then emerges from the bottom of the column.

Module B6 — Beyond the Microscope

Page 150 — More on Genetic Engineering

Q1 A genetically modified organism

Q2 The genetic code is universal (the same four bases are used in the DNA of all organisms).

Q3 restriction, sticky, plasmid, ligase, gene, human insulin

Q4 something that carries a gene into another organism

Q5 Assaying techniques are used to check that the gene has been transferred correctly.

Pages 151-152 — DNA Fingerprinting

Q1 a) extracted
b) enzymes
c) electric current
d) don't more as far as
e) radioactive probe

Q2 separated, electrophoresis, suspended, negatively, positive, smaller, bigger

Q3 a) The victim and suspect A — they share a significant amount of their DNA.
b) Suspect B because his/her DNA matches the DNA found at the crime scene.

Q4 1. Extract the DNA from the cells.
2. Cut the DNA into small sections.
3. Separate the sections of DNA.
4. Compare the unique patterns of DNA.

Q5

	Foal	Mother	Father
DNA sample	Sample 1	Sample 2	**Sample 4**

Q6 a) E.g. DNA from a crime scene could be checked against everyone in the country to see whose it was.
b) E.g. some people consider it an invasion of privacy. / Some people worry about the safety of the data/what it could be used for. / False positives could occur if there was a mistake in the analysis.

Pages 153-156 — Mixed Questions — Module B6

Q1 a) i) virus
ii) a protein coat surrounding a strand of genetic material
b) Antibiotics don't work against viruses.

Q2 a) They reduce the acidity of soil, which improves its fertility.
b)

Fertilisers and sewage enter water, adding extra nutrients	→	Algae grow rapidly	→	Algae die and decay	→	Bacteria feed on dead algae, using up oxygen in the water	→	Fish are unable to respire and die

Q3 a) E.g. oxygen concentration
b) They could see whether or not the shrimp is present in other lakes. If it's present then the pH of the lake is above 7.0. If it's not present then the pH of the lake may be below 7.0.

Q4 a) i) faster
ii) faster, optimum
iii) optimum, doubles
b) anaerobically
c) $C_6H_{12}O_6 \rightarrow 2C_2H_5OH + 2CO_2$ (+ energy)

Q5 a) Biogas = 70% methane
Gasohol = 10% ethanol
b) E.g. biogas containing more than 50% methane burns easily, but if the methane content is around 10% it can be explosive.
c) E.g. powering turbines / heating water to produce steam / as a fuel for vehicles.
d) E.g. Use restriction enzymes to remove the gene for efficient respiration at cool temperatures from the other organism. Use enzymes to cut open a plasmid from the biogas bacteria. Insert the new gene into the plasmid using ligase. Let the bacteria take up the plasmid and then culture them by cloning.

Q6 a) A loam soil is a soil that contains a mixture of sand and clay particles.
b) E.g. loosely pack a soil sample into a beaker and measure its volume. Fill up a pipette with a known volume of water and gradually add it to the beaker. Continue adding drops until the water level comes to the top of the soil sample. Subtract the volume of water left in the pipette from the volume you had to start with. This is equal to the volume of air that was in the soil sample to begin with.
c) i) They need oxygen for respiration.
ii) They need water to carry out cell reactions.

Q7 a) a food web that begins with a living producer
b) i) There is not enough light for them to photosynthesise.
ii) E.g. bacteria
c) E.g. marine snow

Q8 a) the cytoplasm
b) stage 3
c) stages 1 and 2
d) stage 4
e) transgenic organisms
f) Because the genetic code is universal — so the same four bases are used in both human and bacterial DNA.
g) E.g. wearing gloves / tying long hair back / sterilising equipment / sealing the dish after transferring the culture / disposing of cultures safely.

ISBN 978 1 84762 611 0

9 781847 626110

BRA44